A LIFEBUILDER BIBLE STUDY

D A V I D

A Heart for God

*12 Studies
for individuals or groups*

Jack Kuhatschek

With Notes for Lead___

D0589600

SCRIPTURE UNION
130 City Road, London EC1V 2NJ

ISBN 0 86201 708 4

Cover photograph: Peter French

Printed in England by Ebenezer Baylis & Son Limited, The Trinity Press, Worcester and London

Contents

Getting the Most
from LifeBuilder Bible Studies

Many of us long to fill our minds and our lives with Scripture. We desire to be transformed by its message. LifeBuilder Bible Studies are designed to be an exciting and challenging way to do just that. Their ultimate goal is to help us build our lives on God's Word.

How They Work

LifeBuilder Bible Studies have a number of distinctive features. Perhaps the most important is that they are *inductive* rather than *deductive*. In other words, they lead us to *discover* what the Bible says rather than simply *telling* us what it says.

They are also thought provoking. They help us to think about the meaning of the passage so that we can truly understand what the author is saying. The questions require more than one-word answers.

The studies are personal. Questions expose us to the promises, assurances, exhortations and challenges of God's Word. They are designed to allow the Scriptures to renew our minds so that we can be transformed by the Spirit of God. This is the ultimate goal of all Bible study.

The studies are versatile. They are designed for student, neighbourhood and church groups. They are also effective for individual study.

How They're Put Together

LifeBuilder Bible Studies also have a distinctive format. Each study need take no more than forty-five minutes in a group setting or thirty minutes in a personal study – unless you choose to take more time.

The studies can be used within a quarter system in a church and fit well in a semester or trimester system on a college campus. If a guide has more than thirteen studies, it is divided into two or occasionally three parts of approximately twelve studies each.

LifeBuilder Bible Studies use a workbook format. Space is provided for writing answers to each question. This is ideal for personal study and allows group members to prepare in advance for the discussion.

The studies also contain leader's notes. They show how to lead a group discussion, provide additional background information on certain questions, give helpful tips on group dynamics and suggest ways to deal with problems which may arise during the discussion. With such helps, someone with little or no experience can lead an effective study.

Suggestions for Individual Study

1. As you begin each study, pray that God will help you to understand and apply the passage to your life.

2. Read and reread the assigned Bible passage to familiarize yourself with what the author is saying. In the case of book studies, you may want to read through the entire book prior to the first study. This will give you a helpful overview of its contents.

3. A good modern translation of the Bible, rather than the King James Version or a paraphrase, will give you the most help. The New International Version, the New American Standard Bible and the Revised Standard Version are all recommended. However, the questions in this guide are based on the New International Version.

4. Write your answers in the space provided in the study guide. This will help you to express your understanding of the passage clearly.

5. It might be good to have a Bible dictionary handy. Use it to look up any unfamiliar words, names or places.

Suggestions for Group Study

1. Come to the study prepared. Follow the suggestions for individual study mentioned above. You will find that careful preparation will greatly enrich your time spent in group discussion.

2. Be willing to participate in the discussion. The leader of your group will not be lecturing. Instead, he or she will be encouraging the members of the group to discuss what they have learned from the passage. The leader will be asking the questions that are found in this guide. Plan to share what God has taught you in your individual study.

3. Stick to the passage being studied. Your answers should be based on the verses which are the focus of the discussion and not on outside authorities such as commentaries or speakers. This guide deliberately avoids jumping

from book to book or passage to passage. Each study focuses on only one passage. Book studies are generally designed to lead you through the book in the order in which it was written. This will help you follow the author's argument.

4. Be sensitive to the other members of the group. Listen attentively when they share what they have learned. You may be surprised by their insights! Link what you say to the comments of others so the group stays on the topic. Also, be affirming whenever you can. This will encourage some of the more hesitant members of the group to participate.

5. Be careful not to dominate the discussion. We are sometimes so eager to share what we have learned that we leave too little opportunity for others to respond. By all means participate! But allow others to also.

6. Expect God to teach you through the passage being discussed and through the other members of the group. Pray that you will have an enjoyable and profitable time together.

7. If you are the discussion leader, you will find additional suggestions and helpful ideas for each study in the leader's notes. These are found at the back of the guide.

Introducing David

When I was a child, my hero was Superman. Like him, I wanted to be faster than a speeding bullet, able to leap tall buildings in a single bound and bend steel in my bare hands. Using a bath towel for my cape, I flew around the house, performing imaginary feats of strength and courage.

As I grew up, however, I discovered that Superman was not the best kind of hero. I found it impossible to be like him, no matter how hard I tried. Bullets simply wouldn't bounce off me and neither would harsh words, fears, disappointments, illnesses nor a hundred other weaknesses that are common to a frail, fallen humanity.

Bullets didn't bounce off David either. As I read about his life, I am astonished at how open and vulnerable he was. He records his weaknesses and struggles for all the world to read: "I am worn out from groaning; all night long I flood my bed with weeping and drench my couch with tears. My eyes grow weak with sorrow; they fail me because of all my foes." "I know my transgressions, and my sin is always before me. Against you, you only, have I sinned and done what is evil in your sight" (Ps 6:7; 51:3-4).

Yet in spite of all his weaknesses, fears, doubts and sins, David was also a man of faith. His life illustrates a tenacious trust in God and an intense desire to know him: "The Lord is my light and my salvation—whom shall I fear? The Lord is the stronghold of my life—of whom shall I be afraid?" "One thing I ask of the LORD, this is what I seek: that I may dwell in the house of the LORD . . . and to seek him in his temple" (Ps 27:1, 4). Because of these qualities, God was able to use David mightily, moulding and shaping him into a man after his own heart.

I believe we need this kind of three-dimensional role model today—someone who allows us to be fully human, yet who inspires us to look beyond our weaknesses and frailties to the Living God.

This study guide allows us to observe David from the beginning of his career to the end of his life. It doesn't cover every detail but rather selects key events which reveal the multifaceted character of this remarkable man. Each study also focuses on the real hero of every biblical narrative—the Lord himself.

David's life extended from around 1040 to 970 B.C. Second Samuel 5 records that "David was thirty years old when he became king, and he reigned forty years. In Hebron he reigned over Judah seven years and six months, and in Jerusalem he reigned over all Israel and Judah thirty-three years" (vv. 4-5). The biblical writers view David as the greatest of Israel's kings and the one through whom the ultimate king, the Messiah, eventually came (see Mt 1:1; Lk 3:31).

It is my prayer that as you study the life of David, you too will develop a passionate heart for God.

1
The Lord Looks at the Heart

1 Samuel 16:1-13

In the book *Selling of the President,* author Joe McGinniss emphasized that in politics, image is everything. A candidate must exude confidence, charm and good looks. Never mind the real issues of the campaign. A broad smile, a warm handshake, and the ability to look good on camera are much more important for selling the political product to the ultimate consumer—the registered voter.

Israel's first king, Saul, was the ideal candidate—tall, handsome and impressive. Unfortunately, he was also foolish and disobedient. As Israel's second king is chosen, the Lord rejects worldly standards of leadership and selects David, a man after his own heart.

1. How does a person's appearance affect your initial opinion of him or her?

2. Read 1 Samuel 16:1-13. What specific instructions does the Lord give Samuel for anointing a new king (vv. 1-3)?

3. Why did Samuel suppose that Eliab was the Lord's anointed (vv. 6-7; see 17:13)?

4. According to verse 7, how does God's judgment differ from ours?

5. The Lord tells Samuel, "Man looks at the outward appearance" (v. 7). What sorts of "outward" things do we tend to look at in people?

6. How does our culture reinforce our emphasis on appearance?

7. Why are outward qualities an unreliable way to judge a person?

8. If you had been given the job of finding the next king of Israel, why would David have been an unlikely choice?

In what sense was he also a good choice (see v. 18)?

9. Why do you think the Lord has Samuel look at each of Jesse's sons before revealing that he has chosen David (vv. 6-12)?

10. When the Lord looks at our hearts, what specific qualities do you think he values most? Explain.

Take time to pray, asking the Lord to develop those qualities within you.

2
The Battle Is the Lord's

1 Samuel 17

One of the myths of our culture is "if you set your mind to it, you can do anything." The heroes of that myth are self-made men and women, those who climb from obscurity to fame through sheer will power and determination. The message is clear. Victory goes to the strong, and the spoils of victory to those who are powerful.

The Bible presents a very different message: "Not by might nor by power, but by my Spirit, says the LORD Almighty" (Zech 4:6). In this chapter David confronts not only Goliath but also our myths of human adequacy.

1. When you are faced with a challenge that seems beyond your abilities, how do you tend to respond?

2. Read 1 Samuel 17. Humanly speaking, why were the Israelites justly terrified of Goliath (vv. 1-11)?

3. Spiritually speaking, what had the Israelites forgotten about God's covenant promises (see Deut 20:1-4)?

4. What promises do we need to remember during the battles of life? (See, for example, Mt 28:20; Rom 8:28; 2 Cor 12:9; Heb 13:5-6.)

5. As David reaches the army camp, what does he learn about their situation (vv. 12-27)?

6. Why do you think David's brother is so harsh with him (vv. 28-30)?

7. From a human standpoint, why was David an unlikely choice as the champion of Israel (vv. 15, 33, 38-40)?

What risk was Saul taking in allowing David to fight Goliath (vv. 8-9)?

8. Normally, we select people who are humanly qualified to do a job. Likewise, we normally take on responsibilities for which we feel qualified. Does faith remove the need for human qualifications? Why or why not?

When is it proper to trust God to overcome our deficiencies?

9. David is confident that he can defeat Goliath (vv. 34-37). Is this faith or merely youthful bravado? Explain.

10. How can previous spiritual victories encourage us when facing future battles?

11. What impresses you about the conversation and battle between David and Goliath (vv. 41-49)?

12. What "Goliaths" are you currently facing—either at work or home or in your personal life?

13. How can David's example give you hope and courage as you face those battles?

3
True Friendship

1 Samuel 18:1-4; 20:1-17, 30-42; 2 Samuel 1:25-27

When I was growing up, I had a friend named David Miller. David and I met in grammar school. In the third grade we were in Cub Scouts together. In the fourth grade we both had the same girlfriend. In sixth and seventh grade we went to camp together. Our relationship continued through high school, then we lost touch with each other, and later I moved to another city.

After many years, I went home for a visit and decided to stop by and see David. He was living in the same house—now, with his wife and children. After the initial shock and joy at seeing each other, he invited me in. As I stepped inside, I felt as though I were stepping back in time. All the childhood memories associated with his house flooded back into my mind. What good friends we'd been!

In this study we will explore the strong relationship between David and Jonathan. It helps us see and appreciate the qualities of true friendship.

1. What qualities do you appreciate most in a friend, and why?

2. Read 1 Samuel 18:1-4; 20:1-17. What impresses you about Jonathan's and David's love for each other?

3. How does their love express itself in their commitment to each other?

4. What kinds of mutual commitments can strengthen our friendships with those we love?

5. Read 1 Samuel 20:30-42; 2 Samuel 1:25-27. How does Jonathan's experience with Saul demonstrate some of the cost of friendship?

6. In what other ways can friendship be costly?

7. What do we learn about the level of intimacy between Jonathan and David (1 Sam 20:41-42; 2 Sam 1:25-27)?

8. Do you think it is more difficult for women or for men to achieve that kind of intimacy in friendship? Explain.

9. What factors enhance or inhibit intimacy in a relationship?

10. Think of your closest friend. If you could pick one area in which you'd like your friendship to be more like Jonathan's and David's, what would it be?

What specific steps can you take to achieve that goal?

4
A Matter of Conscience

1 Samuel 24

How do we determine God's will? Do we look to circumstances? the counsel of friends? the words of Scripture? In 1 Samuel 24 everything seems to indicate that David should kill Saul and take his place on the throne of Israel. Yet David rejects conventional wisdom and uses a different method for deciding what is right. His attitude should cause us to re-examine our own notions about guidance.

1. How do you determine whether God is leading you to do something?

2. Read 1 Samuel 24. What factors might have convinced David that it was God's will for him to kill Saul (vv. 1-4)?

3. We often rely on circumstances and the counsel of friends when making important decisions. To what extent are these reliable guides?

4. What additional factors convince David that he should not mistreat Saul in any way (vv. 5-7)?

5. Is it ever right to go against conscience in a small area for the sake of a supposedly greater good? Explain.

6. Why do you think David places such importance on respecting the Lord's anointed (vv. 6, 10)?

7. What arguments does David use to convince Saul of his innocence (vv. 8-15)?

8. How does Saul respond to David's words (vv. 16-22)?

What do David's actions force Saul to conclude about David?

9. David could have killed Saul and seized the throne of Israel. Instead, he relies on God both to avenge him and to establish him as king. Although the result would *appear* to be the same in both cases, how would it be different?

---

10. How can we know when to take matters into our own hands and when to leave them in God's hands?

5
Secure in the Lord

1 Samuel 25

In the TV series "The Honeymooners" Ralph Cramden used to threaten to knock his wife clear to the moon. "One of these days, Alice, *bang . . . zoom!*" We all give similar threats at one time or another: "I'll get you for this!" "You'll be sorry you ever treated me that way!" "You'll wish you had never been born!" When people mistreat us, we instinctively want revenge. We want to get even, to show them how it feels.

In 1 Samuel 25 David is insulted by a man named Nabal. David's response gives us both a positive and negative example of how we should respond to those who mistreat us.

1. Someone once dumped a large load of garbage on a man's private property. While looking through the garbage, the man found the offender's name and address. He quickly loaded up the garbage, drove to the person's house, and dumped the mess in his front yard. Do you think the man's actions were justified or not? Explain.

2. Read 1 Samuel 25. What does the author tell us about the two new characters in this drama (vv. 2-3)?

3. Why is David so offended by Nabal's response to his request (vv. 4-13, 21-22))?

4. Even if David's offense is justified, how would you evaluate his plan to get even with Nabal (vv. 13, 34)?

5. What methods do we sometimes use to "get even" with those who mistreat us?

6. What impresses you about Abigail's response when she finds out what has happened (vv. 14-32)?

7. The events in this chapter are deliberately sandwiched between two accounts of David sparing Saul's life. How is David's relationship with Nabal similar to his relationship with Saul?

8. What lesson is the Lord repeatedly trying to drive home to David?

9. How would Nabal's fate encourage David to trust God about Saul?

10. In Romans 12:19-21 Paul writes: "Do not take revenge, my friends, but leave room for God's wrath, for it is written: 'It is mine to avenge; I will repay,' says the Lord. On the contrary: 'If your enemy is hungry, feed him; if he is thirsty, give him something to drink.' " What are some additional ways we can overcome evil with good?

11. Think of someone who has recently mistreated you. How can this study affect your attitude and actions toward that person?

6
Finding Strength in the Lord
1 Samuel 30:1-25

In a chapter entitled "The False Hope of Modern Christianity," Larry Crabb writes: "Modern Christianity, in dramatic reversal of its biblical form, promises to relieve the pain of living in a fallen world. The message, whether it's from fundamentalists requiring us to live by a favored set of rules or from charismatics urging a deeper surrender of the Spirit's power, is too often the same: The promise of bliss is for NOW! Complete satisfaction can be ours this side of Heaven."*

The life of David exposes the inadequacy of that view. In this chapter David and his men experience a devastating crisis. Yet in the midst of the crisis, they also find strength and help in the Lord.

1. The Christian life is often portrayed as a before-and-after story, with everything "after" being sweetness and light. How do you respond to that kind of portrayal?

2. Read 1 Samuel 30:1-25. When David and his men return to their home in Ziklag, what do they find (vv. 1-3)?

What are we told about the depths of their distress (vv. 4-6a)?

---

3. Think of a time in your life when you felt overwhelmed by a problem. How did you respond—with tears, bitterness, or in some other way? Explain.

---

4. In the midst of his distress, how do you think David "found strength in the LORD his God" (v. 6)?

---

5. In what ways can we find strength in the Lord during our times of distress?

---

6. After David has found strength in the Lord, how does he also find help from the Lord (vv. 7-20)?

---

7. What was wrong with the logic of those who said, "Because they did not go out with us, we will not share with them the plunder we recovered" (v. 22)?

---

8. David declares that the Lord "has protected us and handed over to us the forces that came against us" (v. 23). If the Lord was able to do all that, why do you think he allowed the problem to arise in the first place?

9. How can David's experience help us to have a realistic view of the difficulties we might face as Christians?

10. Reflect on a difficulty or distress you are currently facing. How can David's experience give you hope?

Inside Out (Colorado Springs, Colo.: NavPress, 1988), p. 15.

7
God's Wrath & Blessing

2 Samuel 6

In the *Narnia Chronicles* we are introduced to Aslan, the son of the great Emperor-Beyond-the Sea in this way:

"Don't you know who is the King of Beasts? Aslan is a lion—*the* Lion, the great Lion."

"Ooh!" said Susan, "I'd thought he was a man. Is he—quite safe? I shall feel rather nervous about meeting a lion."

"That you will, dearie, and no mistake," said Mrs. Beaver. "If there's anyone who can appear before Aslan without their knees knocking, they're either braver than most or else just silly."

"Then he isn't safe?" said Lucy.

"Safe?" said Mr. Beaver. "Don't you hear what Mrs. Beaver tells you? Who said anything about safe? 'Course he isn't safe. But he's good."

In this chapter David learns in a terrible way that the Lord, the God of Israel, isn't safe. But he also gains a greater appreciation of God's goodness.

---

1. When you think of God's holiness, what ideas or images come to mind?

---

2. Read 2 Samuel 6. What words would you use to describe the mood of those bringing the ark to Jerusalem (vv. 1-5)?

3. Why do you think David and the people of Israel viewed this as an occasion to celebrate with all their might (v. 5)?

4. Uzzah's act of taking hold of the ark seems well intentioned (v. 6). Why then did the Lord's anger burn against him (v. 7; see also 1 Chron 15:11-15)?

5. Why are sincerity and good intentions sometimes not enough to please the Lord?

6. After Uzzah died, David became both angry and afraid of the Lord (vv. 8-9). How would you evaluate his emotional response?

7. Although the Lord had struck down Uzzah, he blessed the house of Obed-Edom (vv. 10-11). What was the Lord saying about himself through these events?

8. What new precautions does David take as he moves the ark to Jerusalem (vv. 12-15)?

9. In what other ways was this event marked by celebration?

10. Do your times of worship tend to be sombre or joyous? Explain.

11. In what ways might we make our times of worship more of a joyous celebration?

12. How does this chapter help us to understand God's holiness?

8
God's Promise to David

2 Samuel 7

At some point in our lives, most of us want to do great things for God. We may imagine ourselves as world-famous evangelists, proclaiming the good news to thousands. Or we may aspire to be great Bible expositors, holding people spellbound with our oratory. Or perhaps we will be the next Mother Theresa, bringing care to the sick and needy.

David wanted to build a magnificent temple for the Lord. However, in this passage he is surprised to discover that God's plans for David are far greater than David's plans for God.

1. Have you ever wanted to do great things for God? Explain.

2. Read 2 Samuel 7. What prompts David to want to build a house for the Lord (vv. 1-3)?

3. Nathan initially tells David to go ahead with his plan (v. 3). But according to the Lord, what have both Nathan and David failed to take into account (vv. 4-7)?

4. Throughout history, sincere people have built monuments for the Lord that he never asked for. How can we avoid involvement in these misguided projects?

5. Verses 8-16 have been called the Davidic covenant. What specific promises does God make to David?

6. Who is the *offspring* (v. 12) who will build a house for the Lord and whose kingdom God will establish (see 1 Kings 5:1-5; 6:11-13)?

7. How do the promises in verses 8-16 find their ultimate fulfillment in Jesus Christ (see, for example, Lk 1:30-33)?

8. After hearing God's promises to him, David prays (v. 18). Why is he astonished not only with the promises but with God himself (vv. 18-24)?

9. When have you been astonished to discover that both God and his plans are far greater than you imagined?

---

10. After praising God for his greatness, what requests does David make (vv. 25-29)?

---

11. If the "Sovereign Lord" has *already* guaranteed to fulfill his promises, then why do you think David asks him to do so?

What insights does this give us into the relationship between God's sovereignty and our responsibility?

---

12. In what ways has the Lord demonstrated his greatness or goodness to you recently?

Take time to thank him for all that he has done for you.

9
Facing Temptation

2 Samuel 11

In *Lake Wobegon Days* Garrison Keillor describes a priest named Father Emil, who presides over Our Lady of Perpetual Responsibility Catholic Church. Every year Father Emil faithfully delivers a sermon on the evils of birth control. He entitles it "If You Didn't Want to Go to Minneapolis, Why Did You Get on the Train?" His point, of course, is that if we want to avoid certain consequences, we must avoid certain actions.

The story of David and Bathsheba reveals how a series of smaller sins can build to tragic and devastating results. We also discover what forces can lead "a man after God's own heart" to commit adultery and murder.

1. How do you respond when you hear that a respected Christian leader has committed a serious sin?

2. Read 2 Samuel 11. Sin often begins with a series of temptations, each one leading to the next. What steps led to David's sin with Bathsheba (vv. 1-5)?

3. At each stage of his temptation, what might David have done to keep from taking the next step? (Be specific.)

4. Why do you think Satan often entices us with a series of temptations rather than offering us one "big" temptation?

5. At what point does a temptation become sin?

6. What plan does David devise to cover up his sin (vv. 6-13)?

How does Uriah thwart David's plan—at least initially?

7. Why are we tempted to cover up our sins rather than to confess them?

8. When deceit fails to work, how does David's plan become vicious (vv. 14-15)?

9. What other people does David draw into the wake of his sin?

---

10. As you look back over this chapter, how would you explain what led "a man after God's own heart" to commit adultery and murder?

---

11. In what specific ways can David's experience be a warning to us?

10
God's Severe Mercy

2 Samuel 12

It often seems easier to cover up our sin than to confess it and accept the consequences. In the previous chapter, David sought desperately to hide what he had done. After his plan was frustrated again and again, he coldbloodedly killed the one who threatened to expose his sin. The chapter concluded with the ominous words, "But the thing David had done displeased the Lord."

Then, when David assumes his "problem" is safely behind him, Nathan appears with a message from God. This chapter gives us a powerful example of God's severe mercy.

1. How do you tend to respond when someone confronts you about something you know you've done wrong?

2. Read 2 Samuel 12. Why do you think Nathan tells David a story rather than confronting him directly about his sin (vv. 1-6)?

Why is it so difficult for us to be objective about our own sin?

3. Why is the Lord amazed that David despised both him and his word (vv. 7-10)?

4. When we sin, how do we display contempt for God and his Word?

5. How is God's justice and mercy revealed in his decision about David's sin (vv. 10-14)?

6. We normally assume that God disciplines us for our benefit (see Heb 12:5-13). Is God's treatment of David an example of beneficial discipline, or is God merely demanding a penalty for David's sin? Explain.

7. How does David respond to the news that his child is ill (vv. 15-17)?

8. How would you evaluate David's method of pleading with the Lord?

9. After the child dies, how is God's grace again evident in David's life (vv. 23-25)?

---

10. The author of Hebrews writes: "No discipline seems pleasant at the time, but painful. Later on, however, it produces a harvest of righteousness and peace for those who have been trained by it" (12:11). In what ways has God's painful discipline had that effect in your life?

11
Misplaced Trust

1 Chronicles 21:1—22:1

W hat makes you feel secure. Is it a steady job? a large savings account? good health? family and friends? Each of these can be a gift from the Lord and a reason for giving thanks. However, when we begin to trust in the gift rather than the Giver, we are headed for trouble. In this chapter David discovers the terrible consequences of misplaced trust.

1. What sorts of things contribute to your feelings of security?

2. Read 1 Chronicles 21:1—22:1. What do you think motivated David to take a census of Israel?

3. In what ways does the author make it clear that David's action was evil?

4. Unfortunately, the author does not tell us *why* David's action was sinful. Why might the Lord have viewed David's action as sinful?

5. Why are we often tempted to trust in human strength and resources rather than in the Lord?

6. If you were David, which of the three options for punishment would you choose, and why (vv. 11-13)?

7. In what sense was the plague on Israel (v. 14) appropriate to David's sin?

8. What are some of the perils of finding our security in something or someone other than the Lord?

9. What contributes to the mood of fear and urgency in verses 16-27?

10. Why do you think the author devotes half of the chapter to David's purchase of the threshing floor?

11. Why was this an appropriate site for building the house of the Lord (22:1)?

---

12. Animal sacrifices are no longer necessary to atone for our sins (Heb 10:11-12). What then should we do when we discover we are guilty of misplaced trust?

If you are aware of any such areas of your life, take time now to confess them to the Lord. Thank him for the forgiveness and security we have in Christ.

12
Generous Giving
1 Chronicles 29

Giving has become a sore spot for many Christians. Every day we are bombarded with appeals for money – from television and radio appeals, from missionaries, from parachurch organizations, from relief agencies and from our own churches. Sometimes we feel like shouting, "Enough is enough!"

David had a very different attitude toward giving. In this chapter he illustrates what it means to give joyously and generously to the Lord.

1. How do you tend to respond when Christians make an appeal for money?

2. Read 1 Chronicles 29. How does David provide an excellent example of what it means to give generously to God (vv. 1-5)?

3. What effect does David's example have on the leaders of Israel and the people (vv. 6-9)?

4. In what ways have you been motivated to give more generously or to dedicate yourself more fully by observing the personal example of Christian leaders?

5. What does David's prayer in verses 10-13 reveal about his view of God?

6. How is our view of God related to our willingness or unwillingness to give generously?

7. David might have felt boastful about his giving. What do verses 14-19 reveal about his reasons for humility?

8. David might also have felt remorse about parting with so much of his wealth. Instead, what spiritual and emotional impact did it have on him and the people (vv. 20-25)?

9. According to this chapter, in what other ways can we express our devotion to the Lord?

10. Verses 26-30 record the death of David. How do the events in this chapter provide a fitting conclusion to his life?

11. What have you appreciated most about studying the life of David?

12. In what ways have you been challenged by his example?

Leader's Notes

Leading a Bible discussion can be an enjoyable and rewarding experience. But it can also be *scary*—especially if you've never done it before. If this is your feeling, you're in good company. When God asked Moses to lead the Israelites out of Egypt, he replied, "O Lord, please send someone else to do it!" (Ex 4:13).

When Solomon became king of Israel, he felt the task was far beyond his abilities. "I am only a little child and do not know how to carry out my duties. . . . Who is able to govern this great people of yours?" (1 Kings 3:7, 9).

When God called Jeremiah to be a prophet, he replied, "Ah, Sovereign LORD, . . . I do not know how to speak; I am only a child" (Jer 1:6).

The list goes on. The apostles were "unschooled, ordinary men" (Acts 4:13). Timothy was young, frail and frightened. Paul's "thorn in the flesh" made him feel weak. But God's response to all of his servants—including you—is essentially the same: "My grace is sufficient for you" (2 Cor 12:9). Relax. God helped these people in spite of their weaknesses, and he can help you in spite of your feelings of inadequacy.

There is another reason why you should feel encouraged. Leading a Bible discussion is not difficult if you follow certain guidelines. You don't need to be an expert on the Bible or a trained teacher. The suggestions listed below should enable you to effectively and enjoyably fulfill your role as leader.

Preparing to Lead

1. Ask God to help you understand and apply the passage to your own life. Unless this happens, you will not be prepared to lead others. Pray too for the various members of the group. Ask God to give you an enjoyable and profitable time together studying his Word.

2. As you begin each study, read and reread the assigned Bible passage to familiarize yourself with what the author is saying. In the case of book studies, you may want to read through the entire book prior to the first study. This will give you a helpful overview of its contents.

3. This study guide is based on the New International Version of the Bible. It will help you and the group if you use this translation as the basis for your study and discussion. Encourage others to use the NIV also, but allow them the freedom to use whatever translation they prefer.

4. Carefully work through each question in the study. Spend time in meditation and reflection as you formulate your answers.

5. Write your answers in the space provided in the study guide. This will help you to express your understanding of the passage clearly.

6. It might help you to have a Bible dictionary handy. Use it to look up any unfamiliar words, names or places. (For additional help on how to study a passage, see chapter five of *Leading Bible Discussions,* SU.)

7. Once you have finished your own study of the passage, familiarize yourself with the leader's notes for the study you are leading. These are designed to help you in several ways. First, they tell you the purpose the study guide author had in mind while writing the study. Take time to think through how the study questions work together to accomplish that purpose. Second, the notes provide you with additional background information or comments on some of the questions. This information can be useful if people have difficulty understanding or answering a question. Third, the leader's notes can alert you to potential problems you may encounter during the study.

8. If you wish to remind yourself of anything mentioned in the leader's notes, make a note to yourself below that question in the study.

Leading the Study

1. Begin the study on time. Unless you are leading an evangelistic Bible study, open with prayer, asking God to help you to understand and apply the passage.

2. Be sure that everyone in your group has a study guide. Encourage them to prepare beforehand for each discussion by working through the questions in the guide.

3. At the beginning of your first time together, explain that these studies are meant to be discussions not lectures. Encourage the members of the group to participate. However, do not put pressure on those who may be hesitant to speak during the first few sessions.

4. Read the introductory paragraph at the beginning of the discussion. This will orient the group to the passage being studied.

5. Read the passage aloud if you are studying one chapter or less. You may choose to do this yourself, or someone else may read if he or she has been asked to do so prior to the study. Longer passages may occasionally be read in parts at different times during the study. Some studies may cover several chapters. In such cases reading aloud would probably take too much time, so the group members should simply read the assigned passages prior to the study.

6. As you begin to ask the questions in the guide, keep several things in mind. First, the questions are designed to be used just as they are written. If you wish, you may simply read them aloud to the group. Or you may prefer to express them in your own words. However, unnecessary rewording of the questions is not recommended.

Second, the questions are intended to guide the group toward understanding and applying the *main idea* of the passage. The author of the guide has stated his or her view of this central idea in the *purpose* of the study in the leader's notes. You should try to understand how the passage expresses this idea and how the study questions work together to lead the group in that direction.

There may be times when it is appropriate to deviate from the study guide. For example, a question may have already been answered. If so, move on to the next question. Or someone may raise an important

question not covered in the guide. Take time to discuss it! The important thing is to use discretion. There may be many routes you can travel
to reach the goal of the study. But the easiest route is usually the one
the author has suggested.

7. Avoid answering your own questions. If necessary, repeat or rephrase them until they are clearly understood. An eager group quickly
becomes passive and silent if they think the leader will do most of the
talking.

8. Don't be afraid of silence. People may need time to think about
the question before formulating their answers.

9. Don't be content with just one answer. Ask, "What do the rest of
you think?" or "Anything else?" until several people have given answers to the question.

10. Acknowledge all contributions. Try to be affirming whenever
possible. Never reject an answer. If it is clearly wrong, ask, "Which
verse led you to that conclusion?" or again, "What do the rest of you
think?"

11. Don't expect every answer to be addressed to you, even though
this will probably happen at first. As group members become more at
ease, they will begin to truly interact with each other. This is one sign
of a healthy discussion.

12. Don't be afraid of controversy. It can be very stimulating. If you
don't resolve an issue completely, don't be frustrated. Move on and
keep it in mind for later. A subsequent study may solve the problem.

13. Stick to the passage under consideration. It should be the
source for answering the questions. Discourage the group from unnecessary cross-referencing. Likewise, stick to the subject and avoid going
off on tangents.

14. Periodically summarize what the *group* has said about the passage. This helps to draw together the various ideas mentioned and
gives continuity to the study. But don't preach.

15. Conclude your time together with conversational prayer. Be
sure to ask God's help to apply those things which you learned in the
study.

16. End on time.

Many more suggestions and helps are found in *Leading Bible Discussions* SU). Reading and studying through that would be well worth your time.

Components of Small Groups

A healthy small group should do more than study the Bible. There are four components you should consider as you structure your time together.

Nurture. Being a part of a small group should be a nurturing and edifying experience. You should grow in your knowledge and love of God and each other. If we are to properly love God, we must know and keep his commandments (Jn 14:15). That is why Bible study should be a foundational part of your small group. But you can be nurtured by other things as well. You can memorize Scripture, read and discuss a book, or occasionally listen to a tape of a good speaker.

Community. Most people have a need for close friendships. Your small group can be an excellent place to cultivate such relationships. Allow time for informal interaction before and after the study. Have a time of sharing during the meeting. Do fun things together as a group, such as a potluck supper or a picnic. Have someone bring refreshments to the meeting. Be creative!

Worship. A portion of your time together can be spent in worship and prayer. Praise God together for who he is. Thank him for what he has done and is doing in your lives and in the world. Pray for each other's needs. Ask God to help you to apply what you have learned. Sing hymns together.

Mission. Many small groups decide to work together in some form of outreach. This can be a practical way of applying what you have learned. You can host a series of evangelistic discussions for your friends or neighbours. You can visit people at a home for the elderly. Help a widow with cleaning or repair jobs around her home. Such projects can have a transforming influence on your group.

For a detailed discussion of the nature and function of small groups, read *Small Group Leaders' Handbook* (IVP, Downers Grove) or *Good Things Come in Small Groups* (SU).

Study 1. The Lord Looks at the Heart. 1 Samuel 16:1-13.

Purpose: To contrast our typical way of looking at people with the Lord's way.

Question 1. Every study begins with an "approach" question, which is meant to be asked before the passage is read. These questions are important for several reasons. First, they help the group to warm up to each other. No matter how well a group may know each other, there is always a stiffness that needs to be overcome before people will begin to talk openly. A good question will break the ice.

Second, approach questions get people thinking along the lines of the topic of the study. Most people will have lots of different things going on in their minds (dinner, an important meeting coming up, how to get the car fixed) that will have nothing to do with the study. A creative question will get their attention and draw them into the discussion.

Third, approach questions can reveal where our thoughts or feelings need to be transformed by Scripture. This is why it is especially important not to read the passage before the approach question is asked. The passage will tend to colour the honest reactions people would otherwise give because they are of course supposed to think the way the Bible does. Giving honest responses to various issues before they find out what the Bible says may help them to see where their thoughts or attitudes need to be changed.

Question 2. Not only was Eliab tall and handsome, he was also Jesse's firstborn son (1 Sam 17:13), the one who normally would have been chosen first in Israel's culture.

Question 5. Encourage the group to explore not only outward appearance—height, beauty, clothes and so on—but also other external qualities such as position, education or influence.

Question 7. You might ask the group to think of people they know or have known whose inner qualities and abilities far exceeded what their meek exterior might suggest.

Question 9. It is interesting that the Lord didn't simply tell Samuel that David was the one he should anoint. Instead, he allowed Samuel to go through the entire family before coming to David. Initially, Samuel used worldly criteria in supposing that Eliab was the Lord's anointed. Yet as he went down the line of Jesse's sons, the truth began to sink in that "the Lord does not look at the things man looks at. Man looks at the outward appearance, but the Lord looks at the heart." The process was an educational experience for Samuel and everyone else in David's family.

Study 2. The Battle Is the Lord's. 1 Samuel 17.

Purpose: To realize that "it is not by sword or spear that the LORD saves; for the battle is the LORD's" (1 Sam 17:47).

Question 2. In ancient times, battles were sometimes fought not by entire armies but by champions chosen to represent them. As the champions fought, the gods supposedly decided the outcome of the battle. The Philistines evidently believed in this practice and chose Goliath as their champion.

From a human standpoint, Goliath was awesome. The text tells us that he was over nine feet tall (v. 4). His armour of bronze weighed about 125 pounds (about 57 kilograms), and the iron point of his spear weighed about 15 pounds (about 7 kilograms). In addition, he had been a fighting man since his youth (v. 33). He was the ideal warrior.

Question 3. The actions of Saul and the Israelites revealed a lack of faith in God's promises. The Lord had promised to fight for them and give them victory, regardless of the size of the army they faced.

Question 4. You might ask for four volunteers to read each of the passages mentioned. Others may also be able to recall promises which have helped them in life's battles.

Question 7. The author of 1 Samuel goes to great lengths in this chapter to emphasize what a mismatch this battle was, at least from a human standpoint. David's weakness forms a backdrop for displaying the Lord's power.

Saul was risking the entire future of Israel by allowing David to go into battle. If David had lost, Israel would have become the slaves of the Philistines (see note to question 2).

Question 9. David isn't boasting about his own abilities or victories. In verse 37 he reveals that the Lord delivered him in the past and expresses faith that the Lord will likewise deliver him in his battle with Goliath.

Study 3. True Friendship. 1 Samuel 18:1-4; 20:1-17, 30-42; 2 Samuel 1:25-27.

Purpose: To learn something about true friendship through observing David's relationship with Jonathan.

Question 2. Jonathan could have been intimidated by David. Normally, Jonathan would have been the successor to Saul as king of Israel. Yet even when it became clear that David would eventually become king, Jonathan's love persisted.

Question 5. Jonathan's love for David resulted in his being alienated from his father. Jonathan also risked his life by defending David.

Question 7. These two warriors did not consider it "unmanly" to express both physical (physical affection between men is much more common in Eastern culture than it is in the West) and emotional love for each other (1 Sam 20:41). They also reiterated their commitment to remain friends (v. 42).

Study 4. A Matter of Conscience. 1 Samuel 24.

Purpose: To re-examine some of our notions about guidance.

Question 2. Everything seemed to indicate that it was God's will for David to kill Saul. The Lord had delivered Saul into David's hands (v. 10); David's men all agreed that killing Saul was the right thing for David to do; and David even had a specific promise that "I will give your enemy into your hands for you to deal with as you wish" (v. 4). With such seemingly overwhelming evidence, it is remarkable that David refused to kill Saul.

Questions 4 and 6. Two additional factors convinced David that he should not harm Saul: first, he was conscience-stricken after cutting the corner off of Saul's robe; second, he recognized that Saul was still the Lord's anointed and, therefore, David's master. David realized that the Lord had anointed Saul, and therefore it was the Lord's responsibility— not David's—to remove Saul from the throne.

Question 9. David still had many lessons to learn about God before he would be ready to sit on the throne of Israel. If he had avoided that long, difficult process of maturity, he would not have been the kind of king he eventually became. Likewise, if he had shown contempt for the Lord's anointed by killing him and seizing his throne, then how would others have treated David when he became recognized as God's anointed?

Study 5. Secure in the Lord. 1 Samuel 25.
Purpose: To consider both a positive and negative example of how we should respond to those who mistreat us.

Question 2. In Hebrew the name Nabal means "fool." This account reveals what his wife later declares, that "he is just like his name—his name is Fool" (v. 25).

Question 3. Sheep-shearing time was a festive occasion. Because he had protected Nabal's shepherds and flocks, David had reason to expect some remuneration. However, in anger he overreacts to Nabal's rude response.

Question 4. In the previous chapter and in the one following, David refuses to avenge himself, leaving vengeance in the hands of the Lord. In this chapter he comes very close to exacting his own vengeance against Nabal.

Question 7. "Nabal's general character, his disdainful attitude toward David though David had guarded his flocks, and his sudden death at the Lord's hand all parallel Saul (whose 'flock' David had also protected). This allows the author indirectly to characterize Saul as a fool (see 13:13; 26:21) and to foreshadow his end" (*NIV Study Bible,* ed. Kenneth Baker [London: Hodder, 1987], note on p. 411).

Question 8. David needed reassurance that the Lord would eventually execute vengeance against Saul for the way he treated David, just as the Lord had executed his vengeance against Nabal. Without this reassurance, David would be tempted to avenge himself against Saul.

Study 6. Finding Strength in the Lord. 1 Samuel 30:1-25.
Purpose: To encourage us to find strength in the Lord in the midst of our difficulties.
Question 2. David was given the city of Ziklag by Achish, king of Gath, while David lived among the Philistines (see 1 Sam 27:6-7).
Question 6. In verses 7-8 David asks Abiathar the priest to bring him the ephod so that he can inquire of the Lord. The ephod was a special linen garment worn by the high priest. The breastplate attached to the ephod contained two sacred lots, known as the Urim and the Thummim ("the curses and the perfections") which were used during times of crisis to determine the will of God. Presumably, the Urim indicated that the answer was no, and the Thummim indicated that it was yes. However, it is interesting that the Lord's answer to David is not a simple yes, as might be expected, but rather the more detailed response: "Pursue them. You will certainly overtake them and succeed in the rescue" (v. 8).
Question 7. Those who made this claim put special emphasis on their own accomplishments—"the plunder *we* recovered." In contrast, David attributed their victory to the Lord ("No, my brothers, you must not do that with what the Lord has given us," v. 23). Because the LORD had given them the victory, everyone deserved a share in the plunder.
Question 8. In the final analysis, this question is unanswerable. However, because we regularly face difficulties in a fallen world, it is important to wrestle with the question. It is clear from Scripture that the Lord's children are not exempt from hardships and trials. Yet God gives us grace during those trials and sometimes—but not always—delivers us from them.
Question 10. If the members of your group wouldn't feel threatened, you might rephrase this question as follows: "What difficulty or distress are you currently facing? How can David's experience give you hope?"

Study 7. God's Wrath & Blessing. 2 Samuel 6.
Purpose: To gain a greater appreciation of God's holiness.
Question 2. Before reading this chapter you might mention to the group that David is now king over Israel as well as Judah (see 2 Sam 5).

In placing the ark on a new cart, David was following the practice of the Philistines (1 Sam 6:7) rather than the method commanded by the Lord (see note to question 4).

Question 4. The ark was not to be moved by placing it in a cart but rather was to be suspended between two long poles and carried on the shoulders of the Levites (1 Chron 15:14-15). Either David was ignorant of Moses' command or he ignored it. Either way, the conse-quences were severe.

Questions 6-7. The Lord had given David a serious reminder that he is a holy God who demands to be obeyed. However, David's fear was an overreaction. The Lord wanted to bless David and Israel, as is ev-ident from his treatment of Obed-Edom. The problem lay not in trying to bring the ark to Jerusalem but in bringing it in the wrong way.

Question 8. This time David was taking no chances! Not only did he have the Levites carry the ark (see 1 Chron 15) as Moses required, he also offered sacrifices after six steps—something Moses did not re-quire. However, David's sacrifices may have been offered out of grat-itude rather than fear.

Questions 10-11. Consider not only your times of individual worship but also your times of corporate worship, either as a small group or in church.

Study 8. God's Promise to David. 2 Samuel 7.
Purpose: To realize that God's plans for blessing us far exceed our plans for serving him.
Question 2. Because David now lived in a palace (v. 1), he did not think it was appropriate for the Heavenly King to dwell in a tent. Therefore, David wanted to build a palace (temple) for the Lord.
Question 3. Both Nathan and David had failed to consult the Lord about building a temple. When the Lord speaks to Nathan, he makes

it clear that throughout Israel's history he had never lived in a house and had never asked for one.

Question 5. The Davidic covenant contained the following promises: (1) The Lord would make David's name great (v. 9); (2) the Lord would provide a permanent place for his people (v. 10); (3) they would have rest from all their enemies (v. 11); the Lord would raise up an offspring from David who would build a house for the Lord (vv. 12-13); (4) David's dynasty (house) and kingdom would endure forever (v. 16). This covenant, like those with Noah and Abram, was unconditional.

Questions 6-7. The immediate reference is to Solomon. However, it is also a promise to those descendants of David who would sit on his throne. Ultimately, the promise found its fulfillment in Jesus Christ, the son of David who will rule on David's throne forever (see Mt 1:1; Heb 1:5).

Study 9. Facing Temptation. 2 Samuel 11.

Purpose: To observe the subtle workings of temptation and how one sin can lead to another. To guard ourselves from following David's downward spiral of sin.

Questions 2-3. The author mentions that David's sin happened in the spring, when kings go off to war (v. 1). He points out, however, that David remained in Jerusalem. The impression is given that David's first mistake was to stay home when he should have been out leading his army.

As far as we know, there was nothing wrong with David walking around on the roof of his palace. Likewise, his first glance at Bathsheba might have been unintentional. However, Martin Luther once commented that although we can't keep the birds from flying over our heads, we can keep them from building a nest in our hair!

Next, David inquired about Bathsheba (v. 3). When he found out that she was married to one of his soldiers, David could have dropped the matter. Unfortunately, he had allowed the temptation to gain too much strength to easily be resisted at that point.

Finally, David sent for Bathsheba (v. 4). James helps us understand the process by which temptation becomes sin: "Each one is tempted when, by his own evil desire, he is dragged away and enticed. Then, after desire has conceived, it gives birth to sin; and sin, when it is full-grown, gives birth to death" (Jas 1:14-15). His words could be an apt summary of 2 Samuel 11.

See Leviticus 15:19 and 28 about the parenthetical statement in 2 Samuel 11:4: "She had purified herself from her uncleanness." Verses 4-5 are the author's way of assuring us that Bathsheba was not pregnant prior to sleeping with David.

Question 4. Temptation is usually easier to resist when we are first confronted by it. The longer we allow ourselves to be tempted, the weaker our defenses become. Eventually, we are so strongly under the spell of temptation that we have great difficulty resisting. Satan knows that if he can gradually erode our defenses he will have an easier time getting us to sin.

Question 9. David's sin affects a number of people. Obviously, Bathsheba and Uriah are affected. Joab's integrity is also compromised. Several other soldiers are killed unnecessarily when they are sent with Uriah on a suicide mission. Finally, as we discover in the next chapter, the innocent child is affected by this tragic union.

Study 10. God's Severe Mercy. 2 Samuel 12.
Purpose: To observe God's severe and merciful discipline in the life of David. To consider how and why God disciplines us today.

Question 2. If Nathan had confronted David directly, he would have become defensive. By telling David a story, Nathan allowed David to be more objective and to condemn himself.

It is fitting that Nathan chose a story about a lamb. Perhaps he was hoping to draw out some of the warmth of David's youth, when he was a shepherd who cared for his sheep.

Question 4. You might point out the parallels between our situation and David's. God had given David everything he ever wanted—and more. Yet David repaid God's kindness by committing murder and adultery. Likewise, God gave his Son to die for us when we were helpless and without hope. Now that we are his children, God gives us every spiritual blessing in Christ and lavishly pours out his grace upon us. Whenever we sin, we turn our backs on the One who has loved us to the limit.

Question 5. God's judgment of David seems to be severe. However, we must not overlook the fact that the penalty for adultery and murder should have been death. David had no right to live, but was graciously spared by the Lord.

Question 6. There may not be a clear-cut answer to this question. You might point out that the Lord never punishes his children today because all the punishment we deserve has already been poured out on Jesus Christ. Instead, the Lord lovingly disciplines us for our good. However, because David lived during the Old Covenant, the issues are not as clear.

Question 9. David's statement "I will go to him" (v. 23) seems to express his hope in life after death. You may wish to discuss how such a view can help us during a time of bereavement.

It is amazing that the Lord not only gave David and Bathsheba a son to replace the one who had died, but also that the son was none other than Solomon, the one God had promised in 2 Samuel 7. The author tells us that the Lord loved Solomon and gave him the name Jedidiah, which means "loved by the Lord" (vv. 24-25). Notice, too, that the Lord continued to give David victory over his enemies (vv. 26-31).

Question 10. God disciplines us in a variety of ways—not just when we sin, but because we are *sinners* who need to become holy.

Study 11. Misplaced Trust. 1 Chronicles 21:1—22:1.
Purpose: To learn to trust in the Lord rather than in human strength and resources.

Question 3. Verse 1 tells us that Satan incited David to take the census. The author mentions that even Joab realized that David's action would bring guilt on Israel (v. 3). Verse 7 states that "this command was also evil in the sight of God." Finally, David himself admitted that he had sinned greatly by taking the census. The author thus leaves no doubt about David's guilt.

Question 4. It may be that David's action was motivated by sinful pride. In addition, it is likely that he was placing his trust in the might of his army rather than in the Lord.

Question 5. This is a strong temptation in our culture. We are inclined to place our trust in our abilities, education or experience, the level of our income, the size of our savings account, or in any number of other visible, tangible things or people. Like David, we need to learn that such things can be taken away in a moment, and that our only lasting security is in the Lord.

Question 7. David had numbered his fighting men in order to feel secure against attack. As a result of his sin, seventy thousand men in Israel fell in three days—far more than would have been lost in battle, especially since the Lord would have been fighting for Israel.

Second Samuel 24:1 states that "the anger of the LORD burned against Israel, and he incited David against them saying, 'Go and take a census of Israel and Judah.' " Therefore, the punishment of the people was not solely because of David's sin.

Question 10. One of the author's clear purposes in this chapter is to explain how the site of the temple was acquired (see 22:1).

Question 11. The threshing floor of Araunah the Jebusite was the place where God's wrath was averted from his people through the offer of sacrifice. One of the primary purposes of the temple would be to offer sacrifices for the sins of the people.

Question 12. Like David, we should confess our sins to the Lord, claiming the forgiveness offered through Jesus Christ's death on the cross. Then we should commit our feelings of insecurity to the Lord, asking him to take care of the need that is worrying us. It is also helpful to read about God's past faithfulness in Scripture. David himself provides an excellent summary of God's faithfulness to him in 2 Samuel 22. We might even compose our own psalm of praise, recalling the various ways in which the Lord has provided for our needs, both past and present.

Study 12. Generous Giving. 1 Chronicles 29.

Purpose: To observe through David's example what it means to give joyously and generously to the Lord.

Question 2. The Lord is more concerned about the attitude of our heart in giving than in the amount. However, it is interesting to note how much David gave to the Lord. From his personal treasure, he gave three thousand talents of gold, which is equivalent to 110 tons (about 100 metric tons). Likewise, he gave seven thousand talents of refined silver, which is equivalent to 260 tons (about 240 metric tons). In today's market value for gold and silver, the monetary value would be staggering.

Questions 5-7. At a moment when David might have felt boastful, we note instead a profound humility. Throughout his prayer, he acknowledges that the Lord already owns everything and that any wealth or honor David possesses are because of God's gift to him (vv. 11-12, 14, 16). David also realizes that our life and wealth are transitory, "like a shadow" (v. 15). The personal applications are clear. If we realize that the Lord already owns everything, then we will be more humble in our giving. If we realize that the Lord is the source of our wealth, we will be more generous in our giving. Finally, if we, like David, grasp the greatness of God, we will be motivated to worship him through our giving.

Question 9. In addition to giving, this chapter records that David and the people worshiped the Lord through prayer (vv. 10-19), through praise (v. 20) and through joyous celebration and feasting (v. 22). Although we no longer need offer animal sacrifices as they did (v. 21), we can worship the Lord through remembering Christ's sacrifice on the cross.

Jack Kuhatschek is the editor of Lamplighter Books at Zondervan Publishing House. He is the author of several InterVarsity Press books, including Taking the Guesswork Out of Applying the Bible, *the LifeGuides®* Romans, Galatians, Leading Bible Discussions *and the booklet* How to Study the Bible.